<u>With You In</u>

Jane Morris-Brown was born in Kent in 1965. She studied English Literature at Lancaster University and then went on to obtain her masters at Sussex University. Having experience in Market Research, Fundraising and Personal / Corporate Training, Jane re-trained as an English teacher and now has a portfolio career as writer, teacher and consultant. She has written her first novel and wraps work around commitment to her family and friends. Jane lives in Sussex.

With You In Mind

Jane Morris-Brown

British Library Cataloguing In Publication Data
A Record of this Publication is available
from the British Library

ISBN 1846855292
978-1-84685-529-0

First Published 2007 by

Exposure Publishing, an imprint of Diggory Press,
Three Rivers, Minions, Liskeard, Cornwall, PL14 5LE, UK
WWW.DIGGORYPRESS.COM

Acknowledgements

This collection has been inspired and supported by so many people, I can only hope to mention a few; to all named here and those who reside anonymously in my thoughts – heartfelt thanks. Darin Jewell has encouraged me in this endeavour and guided me as I waded through a multitude of possibilities, and Diggory Press have smoothed the way to publication.

A special mention must however go to my longsuffering mother; for support on all levels, including the late night and early morning readings that are her penance for pushing me into the world.

A plethora of 'Js'; Julia, Josie & Jacqueline – thanks for encouragement and coffee when the going got tough. Carmen & Graham; for the years of friendship you should have a long service award. Mel, sounding board and fellow night owl, howling at the moon together. Trevor and Caroline – your guidance has helped me reinvent, renew and replenish – you have sparked my creativity in so many ways. My students, past and present, are a constant inspiration; your insight and determination has nourished this collection. Last but certainly not least, my thanks to Murray; for being there through thick and thin – my light at the end of the tunnel.

Zoë and Ella – this is for you – unique and wonderful as you are.

Contents

For Zoë & Ella
With love.

A Change in Landscape

The first tremor was gentle –
She almost missed its power.
Elusive, a hint, a glimpse, tentative,
Now almost
        there
            on
              the
                  brink …
                      and gone.

Time passed. A subterranean shift;
Faults brought to the surface,
Their beauty transformational in relief.

She took a torch into the cave of her
Desire and found, amongst the ridges
And whorls a core of light.

When the final quake took hold
She was ready. Braced. Surrendered
Her Oneness, overwhelming solitude
Became duality in unity
      Riding
          the
            crest,
               Surfing the lava
She saw the wonder of what she had become.

Only Connect

Enfolded; how I love the word – I can feel
Its syllables caress me now, conjure the sweet
Warm breath traverse my nape. Our bodies peel
Apart as sleep arrests us, yet the real
Connection lingers, a heartstring strong strung, hard won
Across the years, months, miles. It seems the sun
Shines through closed lids in darkened hours
To wake anew, refreshed, replenished and empowered.

How could we know, the blush of youth full bloom upon our
cheeks,
The finger-hold of love would come in stealth? That prime
Was never passed? That the bud that opens fully is not weak
 And the courage to commit comes surely over time.

Weekender

Your imprint indents the pillow
Imperceptibly, yet I see it,
Scent the fresh quarry
Of my love in absence.
I stretch to fill the space
That you have newly left,
Still warmed by your desire.
Alone, yet not abandoned,
My mind's eye sees
The echo of my life in yours.
The rumpled bed that holds
Us still together
Bound across the miles.
The aroma of coffee
Taken in separate cities
The mundane tasks that each
Endeavours independently
Make the weekends all the richer.
The jewel glimpsed amidst
The rough undergrowth of life
Enhanced in beauty by
Its denial of everyday
Exposure.
Not in priestly forbearance
But as two flowers grow in
Light, unshaded by the other.
Railtrack, stations, motorways;
Man-made boundaries
To relax within –
Vacations for the heart.

Seasoned Traveller

I read over your shoulder
Just for the surreptitious pleasure
Of being close.
Finish your sentences in my mind
Trying to second guess
The intellect that resides
In yours.
In Scrabble, I play dirty,
X-rated marks the spot, a triple score,
Or not.
Coffee and croissants,
Crumbs
In bed, I like best.
Snatches of Sunday supplements
And
      A
          Slow
               Sultry
                    Smooch.
And as the train pulls away,
Coffee scalding and strong,
Amongst the nameless,
Faceless, pulsing throng
I know that it was worth every
Last
      chugging
          chuffing
              broken-down
                    delayed
Moment of railtrack and tarmac
To get there.

Longevity

Sometimes, it's not the foreplay, two-way
Considerately extended, multiple-y mutual
Gratifyingly sensual, build-up, slow down
Racing to conclusion, that does it.

Sometimes it's the simple fact of climbing
Wearily, comfortably, at the end of a long
Day into each others' arms, and into each
Other. A rhythmic exhalation into sleep.

Sometimes, desire is just there, under
The surface, under the duvet, held tight
After the damp patch has dried. Waking
To a smile. That does it for me.

Siesta

Glazed rosy. Spent, we doze deeply -
Drowned lushness. Rounded to curled
Fingertips and toes. Drunk on nectar
Like the bumble humbled bee, the thick
Honeyed warmth loin rich. Your arm thrown
Heavy, breath musk and ripe. Dusk's shadows
Sepia silhouettes our dreams. Waking in
Warmth, cocooned close-clothed in your skin.

The time for loving – not the urgent pull
And thrust of the wake-up call. Nor
Night-time's habit. Grown great again
Tousled desire returns as the pinked sun sets.

lastminute.com

She was having a laugh –
coined a phrase and minted it
at first.
Your heart's desire
at the press of a button –

                    lastminute.com.

Women everywhere
practised the art of it
suffered for it -
fakers every one.

                  procrastination

The name of the game.

And yet in the not   quite
nearly   there   world
she came to regret
the holding back.

           And at the   last minute . com.

Prime Numbers

Libidinous, lyrical, lush –
Left thirties running.
Wanton, wanting, wishful
With a whoop hit forty
Screaming out for Life.
Scintillating, seductive, searching
Torch held high, ready to paint
The world – not red,
Yet ready, brush in hand.

He saw her, at the edge
Of the wood, wild-haired,
Paintsplattered, spent.
Howling at the waste of her
Grandmother's bones
Picked dry. Guarding
The remnants.

Luminous, longingly, laughing –
Lightened at last
Of the yoke of her past.
She entered fifty
Calmly; composed, coherent.
Unravelled the language
For so long tied to the knots of her
Sex, gendered, confined.

Words that had failed her, flew
Freely, flexed new muscles
And soared. She reached out
Her hand for the man who had
Waited, patiently, at the point
Where the wood met the glade
And smiled. Lovingly. Lingering.
Pace matched they entered the future
Together.

Magnum Opus

Picture this:

Wet, dripping, the colours run.
Puddles of glorious, ever-spreading
Droplets, thinning here and
There, tentative in places.
For no reason, none at all
Save inclination, they pool,
Thicken, merge in patterns
Of their own discernment.
None of mine – that's how I wish it
Free-form, free-flow palette
Beyond words, beyond
Everything.

I long to dive into the frame
Dapple myself with its truth;
Hybrid of its making, forego
All confines, restraint.

And yet:

In the shadowlands, the deep
Recesses of cerebral folds
I sense your brush, lapping
At the edges. Mopping as much
Surplus as the bristles will hold,
Stemming the flow. Giving
Form to the formless. Yet,
Held for a moment, at the drying
Edges, feeling the ridge of curtailment
Sharp stinging tears leak, seep,
Moisten. Not surging, but suffice.
Watermark, trail, pathway.

I stand now, streaks of colour
Mapping my nakedness with
New direction. Clothing my purpose.
Before you breathe dry air on my dreams,
I tap the water at my source and hurl
It largely.

Blessed relief. The image is awash
With possibilities. Your choice?
To pick the detail out on another
Canvas. Or. To share this panorama;
Opaque, egg-shell glazed, chameleon
Shades that bear no description.

Picture this.

Contrary Mary

Flying in the face of Fate, I trusted Serendipity.
It was a short-lived fling. No accidental meeting
Came my way. Frustrated, I took Fortune in
My own hands. Butterfingers! Dropped the thread
And chanced my luck, dabbled fruitlessly; finding
My life lacking, designed a whole new persona –
Wasn't me. Took time out, found myself, looked
In the mirror and saw Time beckoning. No
Coincidence there. Came full circle, conformed;
Did what they said I would, but wasn't happy. Still,
Gave space for Karma to intervene. It didn't.
And then, when I had my eye off the ball,
Providence came knocking. You could have
Knocked me over with a feather. I was right all
Along. He said he'd been there all the time,
But the doorbell didn't work. Sod's law.

Fool's Gold

As a spiked drink, stiletto-stabbed,
We should have seen it coming –
Linguistically challenged by his-story –
The promise of the be-all
End-all, All things to all people,
 'Maternal' yet ball-breaking, ground-
Breaking, breakneck, breakdown
'New Woman' sees all, does all.

What's new? Wife, mother, whore
In one, just add employment, debt.
Why not objectify each other, pole
Dance around the ashes of our respect?
Plumped up, perked, primed for life
At the fast end, dog end; over the hill
Lies the pot of gold we strived for;
Fools, every one. The worst?

Baying for blood, bra-less, battalions
Of us fought for freedom. Sisters?
Never so devoted, we demonised the
Ones who went before, did it for
Ourselves. To ourselves. And then cried
Wolf. Threw out the dungarees with
The bath water. Voted with our feet,
Or not. A cold coming they had of it.
The fools.

Resurgence

Kindled, cup-like at the heart of your being
You carry the homing flame, ready to blow
Gently, fanning the embers into easy life.
Small-framed, yet not ephemeral, crystalline;
The fault-lines of our past and present
In your sight. The memory keeper. Holder
Of keys. Your time is now. To put down roots,
Draw strength from the rich brown earth,
The fertile soil, rest in the shade a while.

And then the hearth will blaze with your warmth,
The nights grow short, Autumnal drawing down
Of blinds, and inwards looking, the burden
Of carrying over, the way is clear. Sharp
Points guide your journey, reflecting images
In symbols yet unknown. Unseen adventures,
Broken bands of what came before, and prior
And ever after. Still in the moment, the cup
Half full and waiting. Ready. Poised. For life.

Catalyst

You step on to the time bomb of your life
Unnoticed, until the subtle charges echo
Into consciousness. Born for this, you feel
The pain keenly, yet know you have no choice.
Your very presence sparks reaction, compels
Response in others. Magnetic, you attract
And repel alike; it can be no other way,
And yet you rail against your destiny, shout
'Foul' at every twist and turn, hooked
By your own bait. Flailing wildly, wanton
Reckless. To no avail.
                                    Older and wiser
You trace the wires to their source,
Ready to defuse your power, dull down
Dumb down, disillusioned. Yet at that
Moment, you pause, transfixed by visions
Of a life less lived, creativity stifled,
And think again – of the chemical,
Organic role you play in others' lives.
Constructive force or curse, your energy
Drives you on to change, transform.
Chameleon, catalyst, quitter never;
You step once more into the unknown
And rejoice.

Renaissance

A jewel in ruby red packaging, only a heel-click
Away from sari-swept shores. Tussled at the eye
Of the storm, toes pinched into someone else's
Shoes – borrowed for a while, lest the flattened
Footstep claim her identity forever. Soft tissue
Wraps the chrysalis from the tornado's power.
Epicentre of her being, inwards, she weaves bright
Colours of transformation, waits, coiling the strands
Of her future. The winds rage, moaning the pangs of
Her rebirth; she hears them muffled, cocooned, safe.

Soon, she will emerge, fragile perhaps, but stronger
For the tempests. Glory in her new form, grateful
In recognition of the new day that made her whole.
The emerald of the city glints below as she soars,
Tantalisingly close, surfing the calm eddies of hope,
Who knows where she will land? Wherever –
The destination is short-lived; the journey is the
Joy, the all-encompassing invention of multi-
Coloured, multi-faceted self discovery beneath
The tissue façade. Crystal rare, unfurled.

Cast Off

Evenly, each a pearl, as stitches together
A garment make, we stand, ready to cast
Off. Into the future, you and I, now
Individual, complete. The odd hint
Of a hole, drawn together, but the frayed
Edge waiting for memory to awaken and
Pull, ready for darning. Each row a year
Passes, speeds up; the complexity of
The pattern knitting brows with
Concentration. Like invisible thread
I feel myself weave shape into your
Fabric. But the texture and hue
Are yours alone. It is strangely
Silent; you clothed in splendour, and I
Discarded for a time, cast off, await
Fresh yarn for a new pattern to grow.

A pause; the needles now seem rough
Around the edges, bulky, cumbersome;
Not old, but past their prime, chipped
By heavy use. For so long my hands
Have guided yours, felt your tension,
Seen your bigger picture, lost sight
Of mine. Hesitant, the vibrancy
Of choice bewildering, I cast first
One stitch, then another, loose
Knots grow in number, familiarity
Guides my fingers and it is done.
I too feel the pull of the future;
As the rows grow a kind of form
Appears, with a life of its own.
My life. Not cast in stone, or
Rejected, but parallel to yours.

Motherhood without a Map

The only chart is hearsay.
If you believed the contours
Of others' hindsight, you would never
Embark on so perilous a journey
Armed only
With the rucksack of your life.

Who needs the world?
Niagara? Never.
White water amniotic floods suffice.
Stretch marks; relief roads,
Contractions; contractual -
Legalese for love.

The landmarks offer no skyscrapers
Although the bungee jump
Of telling them our faithful friend
Is ill is plunge enough
Without the exhilaration
Or safe landing.

The fear of dropping moves
Through easy steps to tumbles
And scabbed knees
Soothed by arnica and magic kiss.
Oh for sticks and stones when
Words fly harsh and fast.

Tsunamo syllables wreak devastation -
A world away from the calm
Seas you pictured for them.
And all too soon they are
Paddling their own canoe
With no help from you, thank you very much.

Soon enough, too soon,
They will search for treasure –
X marks the spot. Unaware
That the same crumpled piece
Of parchment you followed blind
Is in their hands.

And they, like you,
And generations on, and on
Will recognise the path unmarked
The terrain bleak that beckons –
That of motherhood
Without a map.

One Step Behind

One step behind
Like the consort, marking each footfall,
Holding back, yet looking forward –
Secretly wishing to leap into
The greenly burgeoning future,
Loudly trumpet yourself as
Someone else.
That glass ceiling you feel so keenly
Now, will melt with years.
Your life may seem a raft of waiting,
Stepping stones denied,
But in the quiet dappled shade
Of imprints gather strength
To make your mark.

A Bit of Skirt

It will happen again, I know it
As sure as the generational pull
Of sugar in my veins.
A skirt as catalyst, rolled
Over in layers of deceptively
Shortened grey.
'You've grown.' More question
Than statement. A youthful
Doppelganger pushing me back
To memories and into age
Simultaneously.
My mother's voice replied, and I,
More shocked by transformation
Of us both, tugged down the hem.
She acquiesced. Yet something
New had entered; a third
Dimension. For now I
Read between her lines, and put
My words. Perverse perhaps, I feel
Her assertion lift my soul.
Castration of my self in her
Is predetermined. It will return
Unwittingly, when she, as I, hears
The echo of her mother's voice, and hers
And generations prior
When she, like me, observes her daughter's
Grown, omitting the word 'up'.

Second-Hand Memories
For Eddie

I feel I know you intimately, deep in the marrow;
Bred in the bone. At times I can almost trace
Your genetic footprint through my life, splaying
Out my toes to fill your shoes as well as mine.
You're a hard act to follow.

Your features carve my own; chip off the old
Block, they say. Few live who knew you now,
But in my mind you are forever youthful,
Raffish, daring, all the things I want to be;
You're a hard act to follow.

As in a thrift shop, I rummage through
Second-hand memories, looking for
The pearls of your wisdom. A meagre
Strand, and yet in my heart I know
You're a hard act to follow.

I feel I know you intimately, deep in the marrow;
Bred in the bone. Right now, I can almost sense
Your breath against my hair, a brushstroke
Away. An inspiration. Perhaps that's what I need –
What I've created –
Constructed –
Over the years –
My own path … to follow.

Choices
(for Dad)

I felt we chose each other. Complicit acceptance
From the very start; your Christopher Robin to my
Piglet. You seemed so upright; taller than the five
Barred gate you helped me climb, wiser than my
Half a decade. We seemed to fit, my hand in
Your big paw, skipping to keep up with your long
Stride. It seemed that I always looked up to you.

I was part of the package; a done deal. Only now,
In the marketplace of life can I count the cost
You paid for love – willingly. You took on teenage angst,
And slamming doors, shook off the contemplative life
That you were born for. Listened well, then counselled
Patiently. A step – parent in name only, for I felt
You were mine alone. I grew because you had chosen me.

And then we were inverted; your choices narrowed
By dis-ease, congested to the parallel tracks of
A wheeled chair. I know that you chose life that
Day your stuttering steps led you to church
And out again. A pared down version, courageous
Nonetheless. I wonder now, why it chose you,
Closing your intellect into a pallid stare.

The twinkle in your eye, that I had cherished,
Seldom fought to surface, yet as my daughter's
Chubby hands reached out for you as I once did,
I thought I saw a glimmer, of what might have been.
Now you are gone, I choose my memories carefully.
Reclaim the bloodless lineage of love we forged
When you became my father.

Grief

I learned a new meaning for 'corpsed' today;
The rictus rigid, whilst the sick pit belly laugh
Of horror threatens. I saw it in you too, as disbelief
Like rigor mortis crept through limbs to heart, and
Wept dry tears. You didn't know you had it in you –
The guttural deep response of grief – so primal
Passed down in blood, centuries of passion
Played out, curtained by lashes, soliloquies of love.

The gift surpassed all conscious reasonings
Of the mind. For what had passed between us
In those clutching moments, held as frozen
In time, was understanding. The three in one
Gripped by an age-old memory of hope; that
Loss comes out of love. And love is all.

In Absentia

Silent witness, it is all about you.
If the cap fits – I can see the
Shadow of black, skull size
As they pronounce you
Guilty, no syllable of doubt.
Suddenly the image is skewed,
Distorted with anger.
Silent witness, the trail
Peters out; did you leave
Some hint, some vestige
Of another life we missed?
It's hard to be charitable –
Shouldn't it begin at home?
The jury's out, and suddenly
Silent witness, it is all about me.
I look for answers, yet the spotlight
Frames my fears; my doubts
My judgements. Pale faced
We wait, and the shadow deepens,
Coats us all. Nothing adds up.
Perhaps it never did. But you,
Silent witness, in absentia,
Hold your secrets close.
And I know now, however hard we rub
The tarnished casket of your memory
No genii will appear to save us all
And you. The balance sheet of
Benevolent acts wiped out as
The hammer falls. Silent witness –
Human frailty laid bare in
Unforgiving, stark relief - they
Want the pound of flesh your absence
Cannot give them. And so, in truth
It is all about us; witnessing the travesty

Of memory, silenced in your defence.
Lost legacy lingers long – a life sentence
We must shoulder with you. For who is
Guiltless in the subtle art of wishing
All were well, papering over the cracks
Of sadness, fear, behind the mask?
We know the clown's smile hides
A multitude of sorrows and yet laugh
With him. Complicit. Opportunist in our
Merriment. Forgive us, silent witness,
As we must you.

Scars Upon My Heart

I have a silvered scar; it trickles like a stream
Across my knee, like the river I could see ribboned
In the distance, that day, as the wind billowed my
Hair against the true blue sky, as I swung, and swung
High above the trees, soaring as a bird before
Plummeting to earth. I hit the ground hard.
Unprepared for gravel – no playground plush soft
Rubber in those days – sob caught in my throat.
Winded, as the raw red reality broke through my jeans,
No-one could reach my pain, my shock, and the vision
Of perfect landscape vanished. The scab itched.
And as I sought new, clandestine ways to scratch
It undetected, no-one understood how compelling
The desire became. You cajoled at first, then
Shouted – how could I expect my wound to heal
If I wouldn't leave it alone? Give it a rest. Give
It a break. You suffered too at not protecting
Me from my great hurt. Strange though, that now,
Years on, I have no recollection of you picking
Out the shards of stone, miniscule, with a
Magnifying glass, and tweezers. The sharp, pricking
Points of pain. Only the azure sky, and the green, green
Grass. And the breeze between my toes.

The scar upon my heart is newly etched; unseen
The hard harsh edges catch me. There were no
Knee-pads, helmets, no protection, nothing
Could cushion me from this. I have to pick at
The memories, chip away the harsh cold hurt
To sculpture a new form. I can't leave it alone,
Give it a rest. I start in anger, wielding my
Chisel fiercely, prising back the years to when
Hope triumphed. I prickle with understanding;

As you before, irrational, I blame His carelessness –
The butterfingered Higher Power, who should have
Kept you safe. Caught napping as the swing swung.
But then – without the risky parabola, the high
Arched curve, I would never have seen the view
Beyond the tops of trees. A snapshot.
I will have a silvered scar upon my heart,
One day, streaking like the grey hair
That never crossed your brow. And the azure
Skies we shared, and the green, green grass
Will verdant grow. Not now. Not yet.
For the scab is ripe for picking, the sore
Sore. And it hurts.

Hindsight

I supped the poisoned chalice that you held
For me to drink. The sediment hidden by
The flush-red rouge thirst-quenching
Knowledge that filled my veins. Innocent,
Naïve, I swallowed whole the lies, the lines
Lyrical, poetic patter, thrumming on
The web you chose to weave so carefully
Around your prey, my friend.

And now the mask has slipped. The painted
Sight no pretty picture now. The glass has
Shattered; fragments, shards remain in
Lives you wrecked and yours. A bitter pill -
Not mine to buy or sell. Transmuted though,
The learning is complete. I am not you.

Gossip

You know who you are, with acid tongue
Who sees the worst in others, passes on
The lies that blister there. Garrulous,
You glory in half truths, regardless
Of the pain you cause. Uncaring.
You have no name, polluting others'
With forked barbs, high on the
Thrill of 'knowing', weaving the web
Forgetting that its residue will
One day snare you too.

For as you sit proud, resplendent,
At the centre of your creation,
Beware the laws of life that you ignore.
Remember that what you project
Says more about the teller than
The tale. The sting in the tail.
The lie lies low and waiting,
Ready   to   pounce. Ready to
Rebound. With deadly accuracy.
And then, we will all see who you are.

Bully For You

Bruised by your words, I feel the subtle
(Or not so) kick behind their spiked
Syllables. You who know me so well,
Have fingered the soft under-belly
Of my fear so often that the memory
Lances your absence. I experience
The lack of you as a shadow lingering.
It's dark cast worming, whorling, soil
Deep. So deep. It takes me back.

      In the playground the lines were drawn
      For games, or battle. Like a ruled page
      It's black and white. Clear cut. You're
      In or you're
              OUT.
                    On the sidelines
      Warming up – hot salt tramlines
      Marking whispered hissing hurtful
      Time.

But now the odds are higher. The sticks
And stones are boulders and the price
Is right up your street. After all, you've
Practised the art. Mixed the colours
To perfection. A quick learner. Progressed
From childish pranks and underminings;
Unchecked callousness. A ruthless streak in
Business; "Firm but Fair" you say, "Tough
Love", "Honest to a Fault"; cheap weaponry.

Well, bully for you; you've earned your name,
Grown into the skin of it, tattooed invisible
Poison like the ink you need a torch to see.
And now I'm
                    OUT.
                              In the fresh bright
Air of freedom – hot salt tramlines
Of anger pulsing through my veins. Calling
Time.

Pulling Rank

Soft words wound my soul as harsh ones never could.
Cotton-wooled with care, your vowels embrace my pain.
You choose your defence carefully, determined to be heard
Your gesture one of kindness to the world, and yet
The tone that lies beneath them – no regret, no crumb
Of understanding. A structured argument. True to your
Profession you play with words – a game to you perhaps –
Cat to my mouse, soft pawed you know the claws that lie
Beneath. We both do. But as you sit, waiting to pounce,
The thrill of the chase in your veins, I will be gone.
That is my power. There will be other prey to catch.
You will not care, your job is done. You are secure,
For now. Yet I will frolic in the verdant pastures of
Freedom, go where the wind may blow the chaff,
Unhindered. And when soft words dull your ears
From another mouth, and you feel emotion prick your eyes,
Remember.

Judgement

Revenge is ugly. It sneers at you
Through karmic circles. Repeats
Like an uncooked onion, lingers
On your breath, fetid, the stink
Of ages. And yet … what if
You only lay the bait, wait, reel
In gently, oh so slowly? What if
The work is not really yours …?
Surely then the blame is
Shared, halved, quartered,
Miniscule. The skin remains intact
Disguising rings unravelled,
Layers torn apart inside.
Does it count, the scent on
Your fingers? Is the circle
Complete? Revenge is ugly.
The taste is sweet, but who will
Pay the price?

Dead Wood

A slow burner. But then you knew that
Ivy, fast growing, suffocating in its
Persistence, would be removed. Almost
Clinically. At first it enhances; you
Forget each time that it will take
You over. Demand, through oddly
Symbiotic form, that you relinquish
Self. Its lush green offerings,
Pleasing, strangle from the roots
Up. Stifle creativity, growth.
Eventually, as the wood, seasoned,
With tightened rings, cuts circulation,
The only survival is to sever, all
Contact. Surrender the dead wood.
Watch it fall away, amputated,
And learn to live without it.

A slow burner. And now the branch
Leaves a shadow where it once
Thrived. A memory, tainted.
Poison ivy. Dead wood. You watch
The flames lick its surface, charring
The bark. Free now, you
Sprout new growth from the scar.
A reminder of your folly. Wary.
Of the vanity that led you there
You know at last – harsh pruning
Begets the strongest growth.
Clothed only in your blossoms,
Sap surging through your veins
You rise anew, reborn, standing
Tall in the forest of friends
Who want nothing but your company.

Strange Meeting

I never understood that 'quaking' wasn't really
Fear of the other. Until I saw you again. No,
It's the deep down repressed longing to speak
The unspoken, the un-sayable – to confront my
Shadow in you. Dumbstruck I blanked the very
Air you breathed, suffocating in my own fetid
Wish to wound. To drive away the cloying
Clinging clatter of unformed words my brain
Confines. My shaking fingers beat a retreat
So absolute, so final, no going back. No wish
To. Except no closure either. You comprehend
My language through the translation of your
Experience, not mine, for they are poles apart;
The syllables babble, eyes blur, with me afraid
Again, of what others might think if I retaliate
To your anger lodged in my history. And yours.
So I quake, recoil, protect myself, pretend
I haven't seen you. Safer that way.

Trophy Lives

Award. Prized open. The envelope laid me bare –
I recall as if it were yesterday. An invitation;
My reward. I had no place there, yet
Upon the table, I saw one set. Alone. Their flushed
Faces caught my throat, futures fleshed out;
Spliced newly, the bouquet of their success
Flew over my head – ducking, I thronged with
Others to congratulate; a dowager at the feast.
I heard the whispers; as doubters poured scorn
On the union, chid the ease with which
The match was made. The sleight of hand
That greased the palm, they said.

I would like to think otherwise.
Mine, a world of knights and chargers, seems
Kinder somehow. The alternative – a trophy life –
Takes too much dusting. High maintenance.
High security. And yet, there is a kind of shine
From knowing them; names dropped, a glance
Of recognition, then a conspiratorial urge
To dish the dirt. My lips are sealed.
Like the gummed edges of the envelope.
That sits, a reminder, on my mantelpiece,
A trophy in itself. Ragged at the edges with
The passing of time. Which heals.

Sunny Side Up

Yolk bright, skin thinly stretched,
Promise of perfection, poised -
One false move and the tell-tale
Trickle of yellow blood. Wound
Clotting, thick, ungainly. Patched
Together, glutinous now. Beauty
Grown ugly in a moment. Flipped
Over to salvage – slapped between
Two doorsteps – you can hardly
Taste the difference. Yet in your
Heart you know, you can mask the
Texture, sauce it up, but once you
Have let the dribble of desire drip
Lingering, tasted the sublime ...
Do you crack another? Discard,
Try again? Or, with time, will
The re-formed texture do as
Well, preferable even, to the
Risk of failure. The crack of
Shell, vulnerable shard sliced
Trampled to dust hope of
A sunny side up.

Running on Empty.

Pernicious, it blinks at me, winking complicitly –
It and I both know that there are still thirty
Miles to go before everything seizes into
Standstill. Yet, what is so frustratingly,
Tantalisingly absent, is the knowledge as to
When exactly, precisely, the meter started
To tick on this meltdown. One minute I am
Cruising along, content, before the eye catches,
As a stranger across the proverbial crowded -
At which point does the flirtatious glint
Become insistent, dangerous? Imminent?
And why do I feel reckless, pushing the
Boundaries? My luck.

And now the amber warning light casts
A weary glow across my life. It seems I
Have, for years, been running on empty;
Diluting the poisonous silt just enough, to
Keep going, revving the last of the juice 'til
Top up. It's not enough. Only a full tank
Will do. I want to feel the full-bodied
Swagger, the belly-paunch, the over-
Brimful glut. No more gut-wrenching
Agonising, juddering to the pumpside,
The bedside, the long sleep … No more
Pedalling like mad on the downhill slope.
Fill me up. I'm ready.

Carmen

Fearless flamenco, a fusion
Of fuchsia and pearl.
Bright petals daubing the vista
With radiance, moving with the passing breeze
Or buffeted. Tossing your head in defiance
Protecting the gem within.
We feel your strength belie
The fragility of each stem.
Time passes, yet your colour never fades,
Like those close furled buds
You hold our joys. Our woes. Close.
Too close perhaps, for in your fierce protection
You suffer too.
A bell of sorts, your echo sounds the reverberence
Of family, of friends, who for a while
Are dappled with your light
Rose-tinted, honeyed with your care.
In this, your summer month
Hold true, bloom, reach for the sun
And blossom as we want you to.

Skittish Seventies

Defining decade; the one we're told
Loosens the corset of all the shoulds and would
Haves, slackens the whalebone, breathes out.
Lets it all hang out. Dances with the wolves.

Knows the script; won't be caught napping
When scarlet cloaked fate knocks on the door,
Red, like her nails, defiant. *Grandmother*
What big eyes you have. All seeing, experience

Pulsing, heart throbs seen through, seen off.
She can spot 'em a mile off, those wolves.
Grandmother, what big ears you have. Unspoken
Fears a speciality. All the time in the world

Over a steaming mug. *Grandmother, what*
Big teeth you have. The better to sink into
Life. Hold fast, shake lupine the sinews,
Reclaiming the red-cloak, not ready yet

To pass on the mantle. Perhaps share it a while
For the defining decade, where daughters and
Daughters of daughters tread lightly beside
Her. Explore the wood, take new paths, crush

The grass under her feet. Scattering the
Daisies she thought she would be pushing up by now.
Dangerous decade, those seventies; and she loves
Every skittish, unpredictable second.

Hung Jury

You ask me, wide-eyed and guileless;
"But how, if killing is wrong, can it be right
To kick away the box of hope, watch the
Noose tighten until eyes bulge with death,
In the name of justice?" I have no easy
Answer. Like the time, when driving, you
Caught my eye in the mirror and asked
What "Fuck" meant. Copulation and
Mortality; in extremis, as I feel right
Now. At the frontline, backed up against
My liberal morality, I search for words.
Feel your need for stark charcoal on
Parchment when all I have are watercoloured
Hues. Flailing in the bigger picture, I see
For you it's personal – as for him –
Premeditated murder on a grand scale.
Legitimised. And all that I can tell you,
Word for word of life, is that if I
Were faced, in the heat of the
Moment, with your imminent demise,
I too would kill, to save you. Take
The weapon and drive it home repentless.
Mother turned murderess in a strike.

Your nose wrinkles recognition of revenge
But you shake free; and in that simple
Gesture I understand; if killing is wrong
Is wrong is wrong – how can it be just?
The question hangs, as a noose, waiting
To snare us all. Rope enough. I fear.

Emotional Footprint

When boots were made for walking; sturdy,
Practical, all-weather, flat with tongues
That did no harm, strapped away with waxed
Laces – buttoned up, restrained, life seemed simple.
Men put the boot in; women walked all over them.
Occasionally you put your foot in it, gaffed
Badly, but on the whole footprints were
Left behind in snow, sometimes trod by
Sheltering pages in Christmas hymns, but
Largely forgotten, wiped clear, unnoticed.
We track them now; sniffing around
The spore-filled past. Pock-marked with
Spiked stiletto carelessness. We're up
To our thighs in leather, cutting a dash,
Sashaying recklessly through lives, throw
Away fashions; playing the pixie, out
Fetishing the fetishist. Sinatra saw it coming –
Those boots have a lot to answer for;
Now we're told to tread lightly, tiptoe
On eggshells, go barefoot perhaps, around
The issues. Re-cycle, 're-frame', reinvent -
The new three 'R's for emotional
Conservation. Cobbled lives; we're still
Down at heel, scuffed, but the menders have
Taken a walk of their own replaced by
Coaches – trainers the new plimsoll.
We stand in each others' shoes until
They pinch, but still, like Cinderella,
Wait around for the crystal, until the comfortable
Threadbare slipper claims us. Put our feet
Up, try reflexology, ready to stub our toes,
Anew. Play footsie with the future, our
Old stamping ground, until we're up to our knees
In the footprint that we left behind still
Wet with tears. What I want to know is this –
Where's a sensory podiatrist when you need one?

Frisson

You know and I know it's nothing; that I play the coquette
Sometimes. 'Give the eye', as they say. But I only have
Eyes for you. Plural. A sideways glance is different;
Not straightforward. More a chance, really, a twinkle.

You know and I know it's life, not existence; reassurance
That I've still got it in me – life in the old dog – pardon
The expression, but still … able to pull. Not that I need
To, of course. Innuendo's a funny thing – it goes nowhere –

Well, round in circles, maybe. But you know and I know
Cul-de-sacs are a safe place to play. A dead end. Full
Stop. Whilst the open road takes concentration –
Both eyes ahead, your hand on the wheel, and mine

On your thigh. A frisson adds flavour, the starter;
Warming the engine for the main course. And you know
And I know that there's only one thing on the menu,
Chosen in preference time after time – and it's you.

With You in Mind

Musing on mortality, I wonder; will the scalpel ever
Locate the mind's eye? Somewhere behind familiar
Glassy orbs, in the putty-textured labyrinths, digging
Around for genetic codes. Unlikely; it's ephemeral.

I've held you all so long in suspended animation; jostling
Reminiscences in that central dot. I'm marked by you.
Like foetal elbows, prodding my consciousness, waiting
For birth, impatient to be free of my constraints.

Pen-poised upon the page, pinioned in syllables of
Memory, you find your own voice, independent now.
Source of inspiration, released. Shape shift into
Universality. Anonymity preserved. Safe, at last,
To say "With You in Mind".

Printed in the United Kingdom
by Lightning Source UK Ltd.
116997UKS00001B/346-441